"If you want t[...] [...]n your company, every single employee needs this book! The Emerging Leader will refresh experienced entrepreneurs and will give new insights in your personal development."

Bob Funk
CEO, Express Personnel Services
Chairman, Federal Reserve Bank of Kansas City

"David takes the fundamentals of leadership, illustrates his points with wonderful stories, and weaves them into eight lessons for 'Life in Leadership' in an insightful, thought provoking way. The Emerging Leader will help jump-start your journey of success."

Cathy Keating
Former First Lady of Oklahoma
Honored by Tom Brokaw as NBC's "Person of the Week"

"David Lewis provides an aggressive, fresh approach to Christian leadership philosophy. Those who read

The Emerging Leader can expect to learn much about leadership qualities, particularly that leadership must be earned, not expected as an entitlement, and when acquired must be the subject of continuous efforts to enhance it."

Wayne Cummings
Vice President, Diamond-Shamrock Corp. *(retired)*

"*The Emerging Leader* is an engaging, discerning look at eight lessons in leadership. David has successfully presented the essential principles of leadership in an entertaining, enjoyable, easy-to-read format which will encourage and energize you as you seek to become an effective leader."

Warren Pybas
Senior Director of Human Resources,
Hertz Corporation

"*The Emerging Leader* captures the essence of leadership. During my 25-year football career, the last ten in the National Football League, I was exposed to great leadership. From the front office to the coaches and players, teams that win championships have the most leaders. David offers his lessons pointed at the business world, and I find them poignant to my leadership experiences on the Grid Iron. The *Emerging Leader* will show you a positive path to becoming a more effective leader and teammate."

Steve Zabel
1970–1974 Philadelphia Eagle;
1975–1978 New England Patriot;
1979 Baltimore Colt

"In The Emerging Leader, David does a masterful job of putting a fresh lens on the fundamental principles of leadership that have created the well worn path of success. He accomplishes this through simple, insightful stories that are both memorable and entertaining."

Jim Taylor
Marketing Director, Procter & Gamble

the emerging
LEADER

DAVID A. LEWIS, SPHR

the emerging
LEADER

Eight Lessons for Life
in Leadership

TATE PUBLISHING & *Enterprises*

Published by Tate Publishing & Enterprises, LLC
127 E. Trade Center Terrace | Mustang, Oklahoma 73064 USA
1.888.361.9473 | www.tatepublishing.com

Tate Publishing is committed to excellence in the publishing industry. The company reflects the philosophy established by the founders, based on Psalm 68:11,
"The Lord gave the word and great was the company of those who published it."

Book design copyright © 2007 by Tate Publishing, LLC. All rights reserved.
Cover design by Lindsay Behrens
Interior design by Kandi Evans
Published in the United States of America

ISBN:978-1-60462-449-6
1. Business & Economics: Business
2. Humor: Topic: Business & Profess
07.12.19

To those who sharpen me…
Justin, Joshua, Cindy, Susan, Mom, and Dad
And my love who grounds me…
Jodi

Table of Contents

Introduction	13
Beat the Ref	17
Racehorses, Not Workhorses	33
Woodpeckers, Not Waves	39
Boxing Fastidiousness	51
Sleeping With a Congressman	61
Passion or Knowledge	73
See the Whole Board	85
Iron Sharpens Iron	91
Conclusions	99
About the Author	101

Introduction

I have found that my greatest revelations come not during times of work and progress, but during times of peace and reflection. An emerging leader understands this as well—and that is why you are reading this book. Greatness is achieved through the consistency of sacrifice and consistency of self-improvement.

It is the eight lessons of *The Emerging Leader* that have led to my growing success, and the success in the personal and professional lives of the emerging leaders I have led. These lessons are your education, because experience is an education only a fool wants. To become an emerging leader takes the acceleration of your knowledge, something that can only occur when you dedicate yourself to the study of self-improvement. Even Napoleon said, "The only right way of learning the science of war is to read and reread the campaigns of the great captains." This is your leadership war manual. And in this war manual, I will use the term "success" frequently. It's important that we agree on what that means right out of the gate. For me that means a strong relationship and fellowship with God, a loving relationship with my wife and family, a career that provides a high quality of life, and a demonstrated commitment to give back to my country and community through political service. You must first define what "success" means to you. Know that whatever it is that you are seeking, it will come only as a result of positive behaviors and meaningful relationships. *The Emerging Leader* will teach you these behaviors, and you will grow comfortable with their specific application in your life.

The emerging leader first accepts that growth

begins with releasing the desire to simply "look the part" of success. Instead you must hurry the business of getting the bruises that accompany everyone during the curve of life's education. "The way to gain a good reputation is the endeavor to become what you desire to appear," as Socrates noted. Once you master that mindset, then it's all about making as many mistakes as you can in the pursuit of knowledge without upsetting too many people along the way. That's style. If you're not making mistakes, then you are not pushing yourself. And that's the acceptance of mediocrity. *Style in the persistent pursuit of improved performance*—that's what emerging as a leader is all about.

Style, the way you carry yourself, tells everyone else what they need to know about you. Good and bad. The emerging leader learns that your style must tell everyone you are ready...to tell them that you are ready to help them. Tell them that you are ready to earn your keep. Tell them that you are ready to learn what they have to teach you.

These lessons are the keys to moving ahead in both your personal and professional life. Following them will build in you both the needed character and reputation in order to achieve the success you are hungry for. As we drive forward to our goals, we need a road map designed to tackle any situation. The eight lessons of *The Emerging Leader* is the road map to achievement and advancing your career with a positive reputation.

Beat the Ref

"I guess they got a rule that I ain't read yet."

Florida State Football Coach Bobby Bowden after
a fourth-quarter referee's call that helped Clemson
upset the Florida State Seminoles

Let's get this straight before you read any farther:
You are entitled to absolutely nothing. Rich or
poor, smart or dumb, attractive or wanting, entitlement attitudes will be nothing short of destruc-
tive to your career and personal life.

In my position I am sought out as a counselor
or mentor of sorts to dozens of people each year.
Often these are young people, early twenties to early

thirties, but not always. Just about every conversation starts the same way: "David (or Mr. Lewis, if they are really trying), I want to be successful. What do I have to do to get it right now?"

It's not a simple answer. Or at least you can't respond with a single answer. And, unfortunately, it is rarely the immediate gratification that we younger professionals crave. Success is found in a combination of a lot of little habits and perspectives. But I can share with you now the first step, the first habit, as Steven Covey would say. "Before you can achieve very much of merit, you must release the belief that you *deserve* to have it," is my response. In actuality, it is those individuals who feel they have something to prove and nothing owed to them that are passing by those sordid souls, waiting for opportunity to come to them. Some say to bet on the underdog. The problem with that advice is that underdogs don't always *want* to win. I bet on the *hungry* underdog; they work the hardest.

When I give that answer, the person who

has sought me out to give advice almost always follows up with the same response: "But I can't do it because _____ ." It doesn't matter much what goes in the blank. "I don't have the education," "My dad hit me," "I'm not as smart," "I had a kid too young," or, "People won't give me a chance." It's all the same excuse. What it really means is "I want a pass because I was dealt a bad hand," or "I am *entitled* to a little slack or a little extra consideration because I didn't have the advantages others had." It's that entitlement attitude that has kept them from realizing the success they want, but few unsuccessful people can see that is the actual cause, choosing instead to continue their focus on their "unique" set of disadvantages.

The first lesson of the emerging leader is to recognize that every single excuse is an indicator of an attitude of entitlement. You will not become a leader if you believe you are entitled to that success. Remember that we all still have something to prove.

"Leaders recognize that excuses are
an indicator of an attitude
of entitlement."

Dinesh D'Souza was seventeen when he emigrated from India. Attending school in a small town in Arizona, he was short on cash and short on hope. But he made a decision to make a life in America and was accepted to Dartmouth College. It was there that he began to emerge as a leader. He began to write for the college newspaper, joined a handful of student groups, and began to engage in political dialogue. He helped found a conservative magazine called the *Dartmouth Review* that began to grow a reputation for challenging the college's administration, and he began to formulate his sometimes controversial stance on minority issues. He graduated college in 1983, and by the age of twenty-six was a Senior Policy Analyst advising President

Ronald Reagan. D'Souza has been called one of the "top young public-policy makers in the country" by *Investor's Business Daily. New York Times Magazine* named him one of America's most influential conservative thinkers. The World Affairs Council lists him as one of the nation's five hundred leading authorities on international issues. Despite being a poor immigrant and separated from his parents, he emerged as a leader at a young age and kept on going. And he has a lesson to teach us.

I had the opportunity to meet D'Souza a couple years ago. D'Souza is a minority who speaks out against the entitlement attitude that anchors so many in the minority community to the rock of mediocrity. While our fathers' and grandfathers' generations certainly experienced a degree of discrimination in America that we can hardly fathom in today's society, D'Souza observed that the negative worldview held by so many was actually counterproductive to most minority's successes. While he was pressured by peer groups and minority organizations to join the ranks of those pressing for expansion of affirmative action and even reparations to minority groups, D'Souza pushed just as hard for a clean slate. While he does concede great injustices have occurred in the past and some still occur even today, he also recognizes that government policies will never stamp out the hate that lies in a racist's heart, but instead that if affirmative action or other racial preference policies expanded, they actually diminished the value of the success he would achieve in his life.

Did you get that? While D'Souza agrees that affirmative action could give him an advantage over others competing for the same career path, he denounced the injustice that those programs actually create. They remove what he calls the "luster" of his success because he got a headstart of sorts. How could he stand proud on the mountain of his triumphs if he had an unfair advantage over those people who did not hold hate in their heart? He could not. D'Souza's success came *in spite* of any disadvantages he may have had in life. His may have been his heritage and the prejudices others held toward that heritage, but D'Souza realizes that everyone has their own set of disadvantages, and so should you. That's the bedrock of long-lasting achievement.

For D'Souza to be successful and maintain the luster of his accomplishments, he removed any feeling of entitlement and focused instead on the meaning he sought out of his life. If he wanted to affect public policy in America, for example, then he had to make it at an early age into a position of influence. If he focused his energies on crying "foul," then he would not be able to invest the time into achieving the success he wanted out of life. In his case, that led him to the White House and on to a career as a writer and speaker. While I don't know what path you will follow, it will start by removing the entitlement way of life that unsuccessful people anchor themselves to.

Just like D'Souza, we all have "disadvantages." I grew up in very humble beginnings for much of my childhood. I don't hide the fact that I may not have had the best clothes or the most extravagant vacations as a child, if we had a vacation at all. For a time, we even lived in a house with no central heat, as my mother worked two jobs and my father worked full time while going back to college as an adult—two of the hardest-working people I know.

You cannot hide from your disadvantages; you can't put it under a bushel. Instead, that "detriment" is your fuel. Maybe you view your disadvantages as your race, your lack of wealth, lack of education, or even your attractiveness. Among the list you are forming in your head right now, age probably also ranks near the top. If you want to become an emerging leader, then I know you have at least one apparent disadvantage in today's economy. This economic engine is still run predominately by Baby Boomer and Traditionalist generations and is just now learning to adjust to the rise of Generation X and the Millennials. But we can't seek an affirmative action for age, for the geography of our homes, or for our genetic dispositions for intelligence and attractiveness, and we should not seek special treatment for race, gender, or sexual orientation.

Focus on what you must overcome. Cast aside the feeling that you are entitled to anything because of who you are or because you were dealt a bad station in life.

In my company I lead a team of people from nineteen years old to over sixty years old. We face a business that is highly competitive and operates on low-profit margins. We don't make a product, but instead rely on people as our commodity. Providing temporary staffing and permanent placement of individuals from entry-level mailroom clerks to senior executives of major firms is a business unlike any other. I can do everything right, and someone can choose to change their mind about a job opportunity or just not show up to work altogether. Then it is up to me to face a customer who has paid me money and invested their time in a person I put my reputation on, only to have that person lie or break their promises. What a business we choose! I joke with a colleague that works for a major manufacturing business that the machine valves his company produces don't have the chance to "choose" not to get into the shipping container when they deliver them to their customers. Sure they have their own set of challenges, but by and large if they do everything right, then the valves will show up just as ordered. Unfortunately, my product has free will and will just do whatever it chooses. But the rewards are great, because helping someone find a job impacts their life in a way only a handful of others things can. It is a ministry in a way.

I mentioned that I have employees who are age nineteen to over sixty. Working with these people across three different generations creates its own set of challenges. Combine that dynamic workplace with a business that can fail even if you follow every step in the handbook, and it could be easy to let the excuses start flying when trouble shows up. It's easy to blame the temporary employee who didn't show up to work even though they just left your office saying how excited they were for the job. It's easy to blame the company who has hired you if they change their mind or can't articulate the type of worker they need if you make a bad match. It's easy to blame just about anyone and feel entitled to the revenue that placement would have made because you were dealt a bum hand. "I did my part, it's not my fault," was a sentiment that seemed to have infected the staff prior to my arrival. But we have a rule around my company: *You have to be good enough to beat the referee.*

The year was 1989. North Carolina State University was playing Georgetown in the NCAA Sweet 16 game in Meadowlands, New Jersey. NC State had just battled back from a sixteen-point halftime deficit and was facing an opportunity to close in on a win with about two minutes remaining in the game. They were down by just three points now. Georgetown seemed to be cracking and the clear momentum was with NC State. Alonzo Mourning was building a collegiate career at Georgetown that would lead to the NBA, but he was in trouble now, sitting at four fouls at this point in the game. One more and he would foul out of the remainder of the contest.

State had just mounted this thirteen-point comeback into the closing minutes of the second half when NC State player Chris Corchiani was fouled by the burgeoning Alonzo Mourning in the middle of a drive while shooting a flailing jump shot that resulted in a made basket. Corchiani, an eighty-eight percent free throw shooter, was going to the line with an opportunity to tie the game while star player Alonzo Mourning was going to the bench with his fifth foul. Fans began to anticipate the inevitable win as they saw the official signal the made basket and the foul.

However, what was to transpire next for NC State was heartbreaking and still resounds as one of the most upsetting games of all time for Wolfpack fans. From the sideline came running a relatively unknown referee named Rick Hartzell. Hartzell waved off the basket and called traveling on Chris Corchiani. Everyone was shocked, as was evident by the jeers and boos from the audience. Even the CBS Broadcasting crew was stunned. In the replay, the sports announcer made the call: "Nowhere near a walk! Should've been a good basket and a foul. No steps at all, not even close!"

The call was so blatantly bad that Billy Packer, the famous and sometime infamous color commentator, remarked during the CBS Broadcast that it was "the worst call in the history of the NCAA Tournament."

You can be good enough to beat the other team, but if you are not good enough to beat the ref, then you won't ever be a success. You won't emerge as a leader. Life is the ref. You can do everything right and the referee will miss the right call. You can do everything right and life will let you down. In my business, you can do everything right and you'll still have to face the customer because some temporary employee didn't report to work. But if you are good enough to anticipate the inevitable bad calls that will come your way, then you can win even in the face of obstacles. You'll be good enough to beat the referee.

Georgetown won the game and NC State was out of the tournament.

We all face bad calls in life, things that are beyond our control, but an emerging leader learns to anticipate instead of justify. They prepare instead of procrastinate. If you think you have done enough to be successful, either in life or on a specific project, then your next step is to assume something will go wrong and do a little extra to compensate ahead of time. Start watching those around you. Look for those people who make excuses and those emerging leaders who give that little extra that pushes them ahead of the competition despite some setbacks. Who would you put your money on?

It is said that a good chess player can see as many as fifteen moves ahead. That means that in some matches, the contest is over before it even actually begins! The good chess player knows how he or she will respond to every possible move an opponent will make even several turns away. Think about those hundreds of possibilities. Apply that to your life and to your career. Anticipate the roadblocks and obstacles that are sure to come your way, and you can be prepared with your next move in advance. When you discover to see even a few moves ahead, then you just may be good enough to beat the referee. That's the advantage an emerging leader needs.

Racehorses, Not Workhorses

"Secretariat is all alone! He's out there almost a 1/16th of a mile away from the rest of the horses ..."

Caller Chick Anderson calling the final turn as Secretariat prepared to win the Belmont Stakes.

In their book 212 *Degrees*, Sam Parker and Mac Anderson share some interesting statistics about the Indianapolis 500. The average margin of victory in the Indianapolis 500 over the past ten years has been just 1.54 seconds. A five hundred-mile race, determined by just one and one-half seconds. It just took you longer than that to read the last two sentences! Put another way, second place was just *three one-thousandths* of a second slower each mile than the winner. Even more eye-opening than that figure is the difference in the payouts to the winner and second place. The winner, on average, receives $1,278,813 as prize money. But second place, just 1.54 seconds slower over a course of five hundred miles, receives $621,321. Still not a bad payday, but that 1.54 seconds cost second place, on average, over $657,000! They lost an incredible $1,314 every mile they were just three one-thousandths of a second slower.

Certainly this further illustrates the lesson of *Beating the Ref* since that second-place driver could probably find a hundred reasons that cost them two seconds. However, this chapter is about the second lesson of the emerging leader.

H. Jackson Brown wrote that "a racehorse that consistently runs just a second faster than another horse is worth millions of dollars." It was one of my first lessons as a young manager, and one that all emerging leaders must master. Those that I hire set the pace for the whole organization.

Imagine in your mind a racehorse. You probably see speed. You see them with nostrils flared and mane flowing with the wind passing over their muscular body as they keep their eye focused on the prize. The pounding of their hooves makes a sound like no other. You can feel their power and their speed. Now imagine a workhorse. You probably see a slow-moving horse much older in your mind than the racehorse. It is looking at the ground as it toils, pulling a piece of slowly rusting farm equipment. Its eyes are not on the horizon, but on the task at hand. There is no vision. Racehorses are usually equipped with blinders to keep their eye on the finish line. That singular focus, that intensity is what I hire.

One of the first individuals I ever hired was also one of the most likable men I have ever met. His name is Warren. I don't have a negative thing to say about him, except that he was a workhorse. That actually may sound like a compliment, and indeed it may be in the appropriate context. However, with a workhorse you constantly find yourself having to guide the horse every step of the way. Their only passion is the oats they receive at the end of the day, not the actual work itself. Indeed, was I to feed it the same but not require the work, I believe the workhorse would be just as content. But not so for a racehorse. They love the competition. They love the buildup as they dance to jump out of the starter's gate. A good racehorse doesn't need the whip, but knows it just wants to run. The jockey is there to ensure that the racehorse paces itself and only turns on the afterburners at just the right time. They keep the tempo. But unlike our workhorse, the racehorse wouldn't be content passing its days leisurely walking around a deserted pasture. The racehorse craves the fans and the competitive intensity only found on the racetrack.

My business, and I suspect your business, is a racetrack, and the only ones who will make it successful and put on the right show for our customers are the racehorses. Racehorses set the pace and wait for others to catch up. Workhorses work just hard enough to get their bucket of oats. I suppose it just boils down to the fact that I would rather pull back on the reins of a racehorse than push on the backside of a workhorse—my hands stay cleaner.

"Racehorses set the pace and wait for others to catch up."

Want to be the emerging leader of your company, your team, your church, or even of your generation? Be a racehorse. Outwork the competition during your window of opportunity. Push yourself to that fastest time. Each day view your alarm clock as the starter's gun. And when you are in leadership, it's time to hit the afterburners and make sure you hire more racehorses.

Woodpeckers,
Not Waves

"Little boats should keep near the shore."

Benjamin Franklin

I read every week. I enjoy what I get from it. Not that I really enjoy reading all that much; I would much rather watch a new movie or sleep to be frank. But I also know that I don't feel fulfilled after those activities. Reading the stories of great men and great generals gives me a little edge. Remember that experience is an education that only a fool wants. Learn everything you can. I guess that if someone had an experience that was worth writing about, it's worth reading about. I will usually learn something.

One book I read is the Bible. It's full of great stories and lessons. But to be fair, I have also read parts of the books of the other prominent faiths: Islam, Buddhist, and Hindu. But the Bible holds so many great lessons. We all know the story of Noah and the great flood. After heeding a warning from God, Noah spends years building a great ark to hold all the creatures of the earth. A flood ensues for forty days and nights and covers all the earth with water. For those forty days, Noah bobbed about in what must have been great waves and wind. He cared after all the animals and his family on that great ship. His hands were full, and we can be assured that he was relieved that day his boat touched down on a hillside. Soon they disembarked and the animals repopulated the earth as Noah looked upon a rainbow as God's promise never to destroy the earth by flood again. But I don't think that is the whole lesson.

With Express Personnel Services we put 375,000

people (we refer to them as associates) to work every year. In my home state of Oklahoma we put over twenty thousand associates to work annually, making us the third largest employer in that state based on the number of W-2's issued. What a great boat we have built! Every day we tend to our customers and our associates. We are faced with our share of waves and wind. Competition cuts prices and dilutes the market. Mass layoffs create swings in unemployment that destabilize the industry. Unpredictable natural disasters can slow or halt hiring, and our revenue, for days or weeks at a time. A significant injury at a job site can force us to pull off dozens of workers to protect their safety but at the expense of our revenue streams. But, like Noah, with all these "waves" I am not really worried that our boat will sink.

I believe that when Noah built the ark he was probably proud of his accomplishment. It took years to build and it was one of the biggest vessels until its time by most historical and biblical accounts. He also built it with his own hands in the face of opposition and ridicule from the community. When those first raindrops fell, he must have had a sense of satisfaction. He could accomplish building this great boat in the face of those who doubted his motivations and abilities. Most emerging professionals feel the same way from time to time when others cast doubt on our abilities or our motivations.

Now Noah's boat could withstand the incredible conditions: the intense wind and the towers of waves. Just imagine those nights out on the open ocean with a storm raging. That boat and all souls aboard are rocking violently from side to side as the vessel creaks and moans with every push and pull of the waves. During the day, Noah doesn't see sun, but only more rain clouds—and more rain. Without the electricity we enjoy today, small oil lamps light up the interior by day and by night, except for the periodic flash of lightning. But all that pounding couldn't sink the ark, and Noah was confident in the strength of the ship to withstand all those waves.

However, I do think that Noah *was* worried during those forty days of downpour and storms.

He had spent practically his whole career building this ship by hand. And his concern may have been the same concern for success that you have as you are reading this book. Just like when the first few drops fell for Noah, you may be starting a new company, or hiring your first staff, or leading your first department, or managing your first project. But remember the lesson we can learn from Noah. It is rarely the waves or wind outside that will sink your boat. Instead, just like Noah, the greatest threat to success just may be a single loose woodpecker *inside* the boat. In the same way, the most challenging obstacles and greatest threats usually appear from inside ourselves. Your greatest threat to success will almost always come from inside your own team, from inside your own project group, or from inside your own department. You must spend more time developing and protecting the morale and culture of your teams than you spend worrying about external conditions.

"It is rarely the waves or wind outside that will sink your boat."

Coach John Wooden of UCLA was a phenomenal coach. It is believed by some sports analysts that several of his records are "unbreakable" and will stand forever. From 1967 to 1973 he led the UCLA men's basketball team to seven consecutive National Championships. For eight seasons his team won *every single game* in Pac 8 (Now Pac-10) conference play. From 1971 to 1973, John Wooden's team won eighty-eight consecutive games.

That record is impressive to say the least. I listened in to an interview with Coach Wooden recently. He talked about those winning seasons and, of course, a lot of discussion was devoted to the "how" of his incredible track record. How did he do it? Coach Wooden focused nearly all of his energy on building his internal teams, the players, the coaches, and the strategies—with little regard for who the opposing team was, what city they were playing in, or who the referee would be.

Coach Wooden talked about how his assistant coach would joke that after Wooden's "pep talks" before the start of a game, someone would have to go get a program in order to know who it was they were playing. Coach would be so focused on their own game plan, their behaviors, their communication on the court, that he didn't much care *who* they were playing. He was focused on *how* they would play. Coach recognized he may not have the best individual talent, but he did have the best team if they focused internally and worked together. As soon as they started worrying about which team they were playing or what city they were playing in, the woodpeckers could get loose and the waves would only then overtake them. Sure he had to take into account the strategies of the opponents and occasionally change tactics mid-game, but Wooden understood the power of the threat of woodpecker. He could build the most perfect strategy, play every game on their home court, and even have favorable referees. But he could, and probably would, still lose. Wooden knew the key to victory lay in spending hard hours in the gym, working on the team's conditioning. The fundamentals of their shots had to be solid, or they would miss baskets even if the defense was ineffective. Having a high morale based on discipline and clear communication was almost like having a sixth man on the court. The ability to call effective plays because practice had made their execution flawless was critical to success—it was an advantage that would overcome any external factors.

All these elements dealt with the team's ability to work together and prepare in the quiet of their own gym. There were no waves present: no fans, no opponents, no referees, and no media. Much the same as how the emerging leader prepares. In the darkness of their own mind, the emerging leader reads, studies, analyzes, and introspects. When the time to lead presents itself, they are internally prepared regardless of the conditions outside. Wooden's team was prepared too. They focused on what was inside, not outside. That way they could enter any city, with any opponent, with any referee in any other conditions. And they won eighty-eight consecutive times, beating teams with better players. Just like Noah, as long as the woodpeckers inside were taken care of, the waves couldn't sink him.

Coach Wooden faced many threatening waves: the opposing team, the opposing fans, the ever-present media, and the referee's bad calls. But in your career you must focus, as Coach Wooden did, on your internal team's struggles. We learn from Coach Wooden that winning teams build five different woodpecker cages:

1. Winning teams build communication and trust between players.

2. Winning teams craft a culture of high expectation, a culture that *expects* top performance at all times.

3. Winning teams create an environment that demands personal responsibility—starting with the coach. Mistakes are not repeated because no one makes excuses.

4. Winning teams embrace that creativity and innovation are the beginnings of greatness.

5. Winning teams give more court time to those players that produce the best results; this establishes a culture of meritocracy. Great coaches work more with their starting lineup than the benchwarmers.

If you do not protect and promote your success using these steps, the woodpeckers will get loose. Poor communication will create confusion; discipline will be replaced with the acceptance of mediocrity; excuses will take the place of learning; and you will have a tough time focusing on growing your starting lineup. Your boat will be overtaken by the waves of competition, economy, and condition, while the stronger coach floats above every external wave secure in the capture of his woodpeckers.

The lesson is to keep those woodpeckers inside their cage. Let them loose, and get ready to swim.

Boxing
Fastidiousness

"The dog that trots about finds a bone."

George Henry Borrow

George Borrow's quip is a simple truth that reminds us that only through action are we fulfilled, and only through effort do we grow. The great American leader Teddy Roosevelt understood this. I believe that old TR, as many called him, signaled a certain transition of our society, leading a breakdown in the previous formality of our leadership despite his cultured upbringing. He was a positive impact on our culture, and we still owe elements of our society today to Teddy Roosevelt. Roosevelt survived severe asthma and other ailments as a child and, despite the tremendous toll it took on his body, proved to be a very intelligent youth. His father once told him that he had to build his body or his mind would not be enough for him to be successful in life. So Teddy began to wrestle, run, hunt, and box. His body did grow stronger. He eventually led the famous Rough Riders. He became a war hero by surrounding himself with racehorses, and he never felt entitled to anything, even though he could have with his privileged upbringing. TR became governor of New York and was the youngest president of the United States at forty-two years of age, assuming the presidency after the assassination of McKinley (Kennedy, often thought to be the youngest president, was actually the youngest *elected* president). He did not let his weaknesses stand in his way, and he also read veraciously.

For those who want to become an emerging

leader, TR is a mentor from which much can be learned. One of his most notable speeches, which he gave in Paris in 1910, included a section that has become famous in American business:

> It's not the critic who counts: Not the man who points out how the strong man stumbles or where the doer of deeds could have done better. The credit belongs to the man who is actually in the arena, whose face is marred by dust and sweat and blood, who strives valiantly, who errs and comes up short again and again, because there is no effort without error or shortcoming, but who knows the great enthusiasms, the great devotions, who spends himself for a worthy cause; who, at the best, knows, in the end, the triumph of high achievement, and who, at the worst, if he fails, at least he fails while daring greatly, so that his place shall never be with those cold and timid souls who knew neither victory nor defeat.

When many think about TR, they think about this quote. But I don't think this paragraph is the

most powerful of this speech. While it is important to be bold, it is important to be the man in
the boxing ring, as TR would say. I believe that the
next paragraph of his speech holds more weight and
should be viewed almost as a scripture for emerging
leaders:

> *Shame on the man of cultivated tastes who permits refine-*
> *ment to develop into fastidiousness that unfits him for*
> *the rough work of a workaday world.* Among the free
> peoples who govern themselves there is but a small
> field of usefulness open for the men of cloistered life
> who shrink from contact with their fellows. Still less
> room is there for those who deride of slight what
> is done by those who actually bear the brunt of the
> day; nor yet for those others who always profess that
> they would like to take action, if only the conditions
> of life were not exactly what they actually are. The
> man who does nothing cuts the same sordid figure in
> the pages of history, whether he be a cynic, or fop, or
> voluptuary (emphasis mine).

What TR teaches emerging leaders is that we must not allow our present success to stand in the way of progress toward our full potential. Several years ago I traveled to France and stood near the place TR made this speech at Sorbonne, and I began to reflect. Maybe it is proximity that develops perspective. Too often today an emerging leader achieves some measure of success and unconsciously decides to trade his blinders for a harness—the emerging leader who relegates himself to the life of a workhorse in exchange for the passion for the race. Too often, the successful leader becomes the fastidious leader, deciding he has proved himself to those who doubted, and now believes he should enjoy what he has worked so hard to achieve. He trades focus for fastidiousness. He trades intensity for indolence. He trades improvement for contentment.

I believe that "discipline is the refining fire through which talent becomes ability," as clergyman Roy Smith said. But in this refining fire, sometimes we become refined instead of our talent. Too many have allowed refinement to turn to fastidiousness as the success they may have achieved makes them drunk with themselves. That most risky of all feelings, the feeling of entitlement, returns and they wait for the momentum of their achievements to open up new doors of opportunity. Unfortunately, momentum fades quickly under the friction of life. The emerging leader understands that sustained success is all about planting seeds. So I challenge you: Do not allow the full belly of your yield to create a fastidiousness that keeps you from sowing new fields. TR would never have allowed this to happen.

When TR finally passed away, it was in his sleep. A friend remarked that death had to take him in his sleep; otherwise there would have been a fight! What a passion for life, what intensity for meaning and fulfillment through service of others that could create a man like TR. When they found him, they also found a book under his pillow. TR was learning and growing until the end.

A mentor of mine is Bob Funk. He is the founder and CEO of Express Personnel Services. We share some things in common, even though he is forty years my senior. We both grew up poor and achieved more than our parents could have imagined for us—although I have not achieved near the measures he has! We both try to base our leadership on faith in a higher power and in leading by the example of our hard work and ethics. One piece of advice I got from Bob Funk that I will never forget occurred in 2004. Express Personnel was generating about $1.3 billion annually, and I found myself running one of the ten largest offices in the company. Our team was stationed at the "flagship" location because we were located in the headquarters city of Oklahoma City. After three years or so at the helm, our team nearly tripled the annual revenue in this single location. Profits were soaring, we were putting a record number of people to work, and our customer satisfaction was extremely high. It was in 2004 that we broke an all-time production record. It was a day of celebration.

At just twenty four years old, I had led my team of racehorses through a competitive market (there are over seventy competing staffing firms in Oklahoma City alone!) to reach that record. It was an accomplishment that put me in nearly every business publication in town and afforded me great notoriety within the company. But it was that same day that Robert Funk taught me a great lesson.

Sure we got some recognition for our achievements. We felt good about the work we had done. Wasn't it time to revel in the light of our own greatness? Sure, but just for a short while. It is those cold souls who feel their accomplishments somehow advance them into a new class, allowing themselves to get a greater return on smaller investments of self. But that is just the kind of attitude that will end someone's success, and Bob wanted to remind me of that. He said, "David, just remember, *we never arrive.*"

I was given an award that year, the "40 Under 40." It is awarded by a regional business publication

---

"Keep on going, we never arrive."

---

and recognizes the "40 most accomplished business leaders under 40 years of age." In an interview they asked all the recipients what they hoped to accomplish by the time there were forty years old. Everyone had a different answer: *Open a new business, double revenue, travel the world*, or whatever. I remembered what Bob had told me when I answered.

When the paper was published with the award recipients, the conclusion of my commentary read:

> …With a long way to go before he has 40 candles on his cake, Lewis says he doesn't have any specific goal to reach by then. It's all about self improvement, Lewis said. Did I do better today than I did yesterday? The answer better be "yes."

Later that year, I pushed for new horizons by splitting our successful office in two and opened another location. We hadn't yet arrived. We knew there were new records to break. The very next year, we grew by another twenty six percent. More awards came, and as I write this chapter, our territory now ranks number one in a field of six hundred locations in four countries. We are producing almost double the revenue as we generated in our record-breaking year. And we have plans for more.

We *never* arrive. In sports, a championship team wins the season, but dynasties win for decades. So today is the time to challenge your own fastidiousness. TR said to get into the ring. I'll tell you to never leave the ring. That's were the action is. That is where we get better, round by round, day by day. Did *you* do better today than you did yesterday? The answer better be yes.

Sleeping With a Congressman

"People only see what they are prepared to see."

Ralph Waldo Emerson

From time to time, my wife, Jodi, and I entertain with friends. Often this is a chance to meet some new people and enjoy new conversation. But from time to time the conversation wanes, and I like to tell an old story—the time I slept with a congressman.

Okay, that first line is just to get your attention. But for the funny looks I get from tables at restaurants that overhear me telling this story, there is a lesson in here too.

In 2000, Pam Pryor, Chief of Staff for then Congressman J.C. Watts, came to speak at my college. I was working full time for a boutique recruiting firm and going to school full time. I was nineteen years old. After her speech I went up and told her that I always had an interest in politics, respected Congressman Watts, and wanted to come to work for them in Washington. She gave me a card. I put in an application for a summer internship. I called their office every other day for weeks until the internship coordinator relented more than accepting me. But the job was mine. An example of persistence, but not the point of this lesson.

At the time J.C. Watts represented Oklahoma's fourth congressional district and was just elected Chairman of the Republican Conference. I was to be a lowly intern, a job that paid nothing … except for experience and exposure. Luckily, my employer at the time agreed to "sponsor" me for a few months so I wouldn't go hungry.

My aunt had a friend from her college days that lived in the area. The friend, and her husband, let me stay in their basement for a couple nights when I first arrived until they could introduce me to a family with whom they attended church and would let me stay in a spare bedroom for a couple months. It was over an hour commute each way every day to my office on Capitol Hill, but all I had to do was trade some yard work for free rent. After several summers of mowing lawns during high school, I was somewhat qualified for this exchange.

The job was twelve-hour days making a lot of copies, a lot of coffee, and certainly a lot of mistakes. At one point I even misplaced an important research file on Elian Gonzales, the kid from Cuba who was the subject of a high-profile custody battle. The research took days to compile and was to be used as the backbone for a newspaper article authored by the congressman, an article that was due in a matter of hours. I think they were still looking for that research file when the congressman retired. In spite of those mistakes, my hard work paid off and I got a break. The head of the congressman's fundraising operations needed some extra help. I met the fundraising director and got the job. So three days a week I would work in the American Renewal PAC's office (which was the basement of Executive Director Jody Thomas' house) and two days a week I would work at the office on Capitol Hill. I made two hundred dollars a week, and Jody Thomas would let me stay in her upstairs guest room…my commute just shortened to one staircase instead of one hour.

After a period of time, Oklahoma called me back. My internship had officially ended, and I couldn't survive on my minimalist salary. The long hours were taking a toll, and I felt that I had achieved just about all I could without coming on staff as a legislative assistant. I figured it was only a matter of time before I got myself in trouble. At one point I met notable pollster Frank Luntz, an interesting guy, but one who talked me and another starving intern into helping him with a project. We were to pose as Democrat interns and talk the office of Senate Minority Leader Tom Daschle into handing over some props they were using for a press conference later that day so the Republicans would know in advance what they were going to say. Nothing illegal by any means, but even though we were successful, I don't think I have a covert CIA career in my future. I think we got paid fifty dollars each for our handiwork, and the starving interns got to eat a good dinner that night! For the nineteen-year-old kid from Middle America, I had learned a lot. But my biggest lesson was just approaching, and it came in two parts.

I have always been intimidated. I have spent much of my career with individuals older than myself, and I still have, to this day, a "baby face" (I'll wait so you can fulfill the impulse to turn to the back cover and see for yourself). In high school and college I often felt inferior because I looked so much younger than everyone else. Growing up poor didn't help either. So whatever the cause, I was easily intimidated, until I lived in Washington D.C. You see, with my boss serving as Chairman of the Republican Conference, he had to run regular meetings with the entire Republican leadership delegation. Once I was invited to help pour coffee and keep the donuts stocked during one of these meetings. What a sight. I was nineteen, standing in a room with the giants of my life. In the same private room with me were some of the most powerful men of our nation. And it wasn't just the giants, but it was the ghosts. The men who had been there before, Tip O'Neill, Sam Rayburn, and Henry Clay. But that little intimidated kid saw something that day. Speaker of the House Dennis Hastart was in the room too. Now Speaker Hastart wasn't known to be a marathon runner. He was a bit overweight, although still refined in his appearance when you stood before him. Partway through the mostly informal meeting, I looked over to see the Speaker eating a donut. Not just any donut, but one with bright red jelly filling. The white powdered sugar was all over his face and the red filling was on his chin. Looking for a napkin, the Speaker of our House of Representatives looked more like my little brother in elementary school than one of the most powerful men in the nation. And then something popped. He once *was* my little brother in elementary school. He once was the nineteen-year-old kid standing intimidated in the corner of the room, wondering if he was being judged on how well he kept the coffee brewing. And now, he was that same guy, just a little older. The intimidation left me. The respect for the man, the institution, and the position remained, but the intimidation left. Those who surround me are not superhuman; they like jelly donuts just like I do.

In your life you often find the intimidation in the presence of those who you most aspire to become, but often the key to realizing that aspiration is to internally see yourself on the same plane as those figures. Maintain your respect for them, but recognize that you are their equal. The greatest agent for leveling the playing field in life is your internal perceptions of worth outwardly manifested through confident behavior. But be careful to balance over-extending outward confidence with the internal mental security that you belong as the leader. Do that, and you will witness others begin to fall in to support you as you act with the power of confident humility and self-aware decisions.

"The greatest agent for leveling the playing field in life is your internal perceptions of worth outwardly manifested through confident behavior."

Several weeks after the morning coffee with the Speaker of the House and friends, I was asked to accompany Congressman Watts and Senator Lindsey Graham on a trip to South Carolina for a speaking engagement. I was Congressman Watts' "body man," the guy who would step in if someone caught the congressman in a conversation for too long. I would step and say "Excuse me, Congressman. May I introduce you to Mr. and Mrs. Smith?" Then I would hand the first person a card and ask that they call us if we could ever be of help. Sure he had security, too, but I was to be the bad guy so that the congressman could shake everyone's hand without being rude with his expedience. However, due to a freak summer storm, we were grounded in Washington. Our charter plane sat outside for hours, waiting on the weather to pass. Eventually it did, and we finally saw the start of our long day as our plane departed Washington for South Carolina. After several appearances and speeches, it was finally time to leave South Carolina. However, because our arrival was so late, we didn't depart the state until nearly midnight. Certainly both the congressman and I were tired. Our flight was scheduled to go on to Oklahoma City so the congressman could enjoy the weekend with his family. As we boarded the plane, both our eyes sagged. Since it was just the two of us on the small jet, we both found a place to stretch out. Within a few minutes we were both sleeping next to each other on the cramped plane.

After an hour or two the cold woke me. The plane was probably worth one or two million dollars, but it apparently didn't come fully stocked for that price. With no pillows or blankets on the plane, I was at the mercy of the altitude, and it was chilly. I looked next to me to see the congressman still asleep and lying in the fetal position, his suit jacket off and laid over him like a small blanket.

All these men of stature were just plain men. Speaker Hastart was overweight and liked donuts. Congressman Watts got cold just like I did. Sure, I have been intimidated since the day I "slept with a congressman," but when that happens I think back to these stories. I get a small smile on my face, and the intimidation seems to melt away.

Those of us who have faced obstacles in life often develop the same feeling of insecurity I felt prior to my time with Congressman Watts and Speaker Hastert. Those obstacles and those feelings are common and certainly not unique to me or to you. Those who become emerging leaders learn to use the obstacles of our past, and often those obstacles in our present, as our fuel. It is up to us individually to decide if we are a victim or if we are a victor. Those who resolve to be a victor can take confidence that those emerged leaders whom we are intimidated by are inherently no better than us. We are all equals in our opportunity. Although each faces their own disadvantages and obstacles, the emerging leader's internal resolve, their internal "fire" created by the desire to overcome disadvantages, actually creates an advantage for success. Those with disadvantages, as D'Souza also reminded us, often have the greatest *passion* to overcome. You just must choose to be a victor and recognize that our very intimidation is in fact the kindling of our fire of opportunity.

Passion or Knowledge

"Bankers are just like anybody else, except richer."

Ogden Nash

Burns Hargis probably wouldn't laugh at that quote since he is Vice Chairman of Bank of Oklahoma. He holds an undergraduate degree in accounting and a law degree. He is a Fellow of the American Bar Foundation. After practicing law for twenty-eight years, he is included in the publications "Who's Who in American Law" and "The Best Lawyers in America."

Hargis is also an award-winning television commentator. He appears weekly with sparring partner,

Mike Turpen, on the award-winning television program "Flashpoint."

It was from this man that I received one of the best pieces of advice of my life. This now middle-aged gentleman of stature became an emerging leader who even rose to become a candidate for the office of Governor of Oklahoma. Many people consider him a community steward and a leadership mentor. I suppose that is why he was brought in as a speaker to a leadership development program in which I was participating.

I admittedly did not find much revelation in his discourse on leadership. He hit the standard high points of a leader: integrity, hard work, and character. But it was not until the end of his scheduled time that an impromptu question stimulated the valuable advice I received that day. A hand from the back of the room signaled the question: How do you define leadership? Hargis responded after a brief moment of reflection:

Leadership is influence. People are influenced by one of two things, knowledge or passion. So therefore, leaders are created by their passion, or by their knowledge. Because people will defer to passion, and people will defer to knowledge.

The lesson is that leadership is *deference.* One example is how we, the American people, defer our decision making to the government. How do we spend our tax dollars, or where do our roads get built, or what helicopter should our military buy? It is our political leaders that will decide. Just like on sports teams, we defer to the captain or the coach. In regards to our health, we defer to doctors. So what makes us defer to these people?

The doctor is knowledgeable—they know more than we do, so we trust them to heal us.

The coach is passionate—she is animated as she runs up and down the sidelines. We are inspired to win.

The political leader is knowledgeable—it is the

political leader who knows how to make things happen in the haze of Washington.

The pastor is knowledgeable and passionate—for each week they teach us and offer us counsel or advice. We believe they care about us.

The friend is knowledgeable and passionate—our closest friend is our advisor. We look to them for guidance based on their experience. They know us closely and care about our well being.

The author is knowledgeable—you read because you feel the author must have insight you do not.

"People defer only to those they trust are more knowledgeable or passionate than they are."

Leadership and authority to influence others is in reality just the deferring of responsibility or decision making to another person or group of people. We defer only to those we trust are more knowledgeable or passionate than ourselves. That's why I let my wife handle the checkbook! Often we do this subconsciously because they hold a title or a position. But more important than the title is that when someone else's knowledge exceeds our own, they become the expert (like the doctor, lawyer, or manager). When someone's passion exceeds our own, they inspire us to become better than we are (like the sports coach or the pastor or a great boss). These are the people we follow, but it also demonstrates to us how to become leaders ourselves.

However, there is another level of leadership beyond that of passion or knowledge. The most effective leaders are those that can infuse passion *and* knowledge. Mark Sanborn, the accomplished speaker and bestselling author of *The Fred Factor*, helped me identify this level of leadership when he reminded me of a challenge Ben Franklin once gave. Franklin, one of America's greatest leaders, said on the subject, "If passion drives you, let reason hold the reigns." When we are passionate, we also must allow our knowledge to temper emotion. But we can also become prisoners of our analytical side too. I myself am prone to over think simple solutions, a great talent for wasting time, but a talent that has not much use beyond that. I think Old Ben would have also agreed that when our intellect stalls us, it is up to our passion to stimulate action.

Leadership is about passion *and* knowledge, because people will defer to passion and people will defer to knowledge.

Let me tell you about a passionate man who was also a lifelong student of his craft. General George S. Patton. General Patton knew about passion. Many know of General Patton from the 1970 movie in which George C. Scott portrayed the man. It was written that Patton was more patriotic than Uncle Sam on the Fourth of July. He was *passionate.* You need to look no farther than the opening scene of the movie in which Scott delivers a monologue in equal style to the general. The same passion exudes from Patton's original writings as well. Many of his soldiers loved him, but many hated him at the same time. But they certainly followed him. He believed in boldness, had great faith in our troops, and he is the man whose confidence inspired others like no other American general during World War II. When we imagine Patton, we imagine passion. He is known not for his tactical brilliance but for the inspiration he gave his troops. In actuality, he was known for charging head first into situations where others wanted to build complex tactics. But his soldiers would follow, and his soldiers would fight. That is the power of passion.

The General, however, also knew the power of knowledge, knowledge he sought to gain through study and reflection. He graduated from West Point Military Academy and was a pervasive note taker. At one point in his studies, Patton cited the notable military commander Napoleon in his notebook, who said, "The only right way of learning the science of war is to read and reread the campaigns of the great captains." Patton knew what Napoleon meant: The greatest leaders are those who understand their craft. Weather you are a military general, a staffing director, or an emerging leader, study those great leaders around you. Gain their knowledge and grow passionate in your craft—that is the work required to develop as a leader. Because "leadership is influence," as John Maxwell taught us, but the only way to gain influence is the credibility established by the perception (hopefully correct) that you hold knowledge and passion greater than those you seek to lead.

Recently, I watched a question-and-answer session with Bill Gates, of Microsoft fame, and Warren Buffet, of Berkshire-Hathaway fame. Now neither Gates nor Buffet are known as great communicators of history. Gates is admittedly still a nerd, and Buffet, who has lived in the same modest house for over forty years, could just as easily be a retired high school principal as a billionaire investor. Neither exudes extroverted passion. However, the room was packed to the brim with people that evening for the question-and-answer session. It was packed because people wanted to momentarily share in their brilliance, to capture some of their knowledge.

A commonly understood investment rule in this modern age is diversification. You never want your 401(k) or other investments to be too focused on a single company. That is the concept behind mutual funds—investing in dozens or even hundreds of companies with a single purchase. Instant diversification. Warren Buffet breaks that rule. He has made a fortune (a *single share* of Bershire-Hathaway stock currently trades for over $105,000...that's not a typo!) for himself and others by avoiding diversification. After weeding out hundreds of others, he finds individual companies that are primed to grow. He analyzes every conceivable variable—the managers, their financial position, product development, competitors, and more. If he were to invest in a mutual fund, he would only get the return everyone else gets—an average of a bunch of companies he did not personally choose. By avoiding diversification and investing in single companies that he has personally vetted, he has made billions of dollars. So why do people spend $100,000 or more for a single share of stock and stand in a crowded room just to hear him speak? It's his knowledge. By most any account he knows as much about investing as anyone in the world. If you need more proof, this year he was ranked by *Forbes Magazine* as the second richest man in America, right behind his friend Bill Gates.

That's not to say that Buffet has never made a bad investment. I read that he recently lost over $1 billion on a single investment decision. Interestingly enough, that night at the forum he was asked if he ever made any investment decisions that he regretted. "Sure," Buffet replied, but he added that although he made investment decisions that lost some money, it was the opportunities that he missed because he did nothing that he really regretted.

The emerging professional understands that a bad decision can at least teach you a lesson and build your knowledge, but, as Buffet knows, no decision is the greatest sin of all. Grow passionate and increase your knowledge. You will create the confidence to make sound decisions. Others will defer and you will grow. A leader emerges through the soil of passion or the soil of knowledge.

See the Whole Board

"Vision is the art of seeing things invisible."

Jonathan Swift

All our interactions with people are connected. There is an adage in Washington D.C. about political power. The belief is that there is a finite amount of this power (better described as influence). When someone is gaining power, then someone else is losing power. The same concept applies in your career.

There is also an old lesson taught to young trial lawyers. That is, when you are questioning a witness, you never ask a question to which you do not already know how the witness will answer. They are taught the lesson of "seeing the whole board." They are taught to understand the domino effect of asking a question, the answer that will be given, and how that answer will sway the opinion of the judge or jury. They learn to see that entire board before they ever ask the first question.

An acquaintance from high school, David Holt, found himself working in the White House a couple years after college. I traveled to D.C. to visit a friend who was working in the office of Vice President Dick Cheney, and David gave us both a personal tour of the White House. It is actually a very old building that can show its age when you are up close. I was completely awestruck when we were able to walk on the promenade that passes in front of the Rose Garden and connects to the Oval Office. Looking out between those white columns across the perfectly manicured lawn and watching tourists looking back at us made me appreciate the awesome expectations we have of the presidency.

We expect this single person to "watch the board" for us, to know what is going on in all parts of the world at all times and, more importantly, to anticipate problems before they arise.

The West Wing was a TV drama following the life of President Joseph Bartlett and his staff. In one episode the president (played by Martin Sheen) was overcoming that week's impossible situation and used a chess analogy to warn a member of his staff not to focus too narrowly when making decision. "You must see the whole board," he said. Just like in chess, if your piece is threatened, you don't expose your king in order to protect a pawn. You watch the whole board and learn that it is the great chess player, and great leader, that can see several moves ahead.

Remember the great chess player from the first chapter? The one who can see fifteen or more moves ahead? This lesson is where he was born. The game of chess begins on a board with sixty-four squares. Each of the two players controls sixteen pieces set out on pre-designated spaces on the board. The game begins with white moving either a pawn or a knight for a total of twenty possible opening moves. Likewise, black is limited on their first turn to the same twenty possible moves. The number of possible moves balloons exponentially afterwards. Game theorists and mathematicians are not completely sure how many possible chess games there are under the rules of the game, but let's suffice to say that there are at least several million potential combinations of moves in the game of chess. According to the international governing body of professional chess players, FIDE—*Fedération Internationale des Échecs*—there are approximately thirty thousand chess players with an international rating. Within that group, the upper echelon represents the truly "great" chess players. They can make a move and know in advance what likely move their opponent will make in response. In turn, they know what move they will make and their opponent's most logical second turn as a result. Millions of potential combinations, but the great chess players can affect the tempo and direction of the game through their vision of the whole board.

Not just in a three-dimensional space, but in the fourth dimension—time. They know the cascade of actions that will come from each move they make.

Great leaders are ones who can see how their actions or their "moves" will impact the actions of others and the other domino effects their actions will create. I believe this is the true definition of vision, the art of seeing things invisible to the eye, but visible to the mind. While one important factor to remember is how to "beat the ref" by anticipating what negative things will happen, it is just as important to learn how your actions will influence the actions of others, both positive and negative. You plan for the worst, but seeing the whole board is about choosing the best path in a world of infinite variables.

The emerging leader becomes a student of himself, learning how his actions affect the whole board, while growing from each decision, both significant and trivial. Your study begins now by thinking in hindsight about recent decisions and how they affected your situation for the positive and negative. What results did you not anticipate? What was the response of those people around you who were affected by your actions?

Iron Sharpens Iron

"Iron sharpens iron, so one man sharpens another."

Proverbs 27:17 (NASB)

I was married to the love of my life in 2006. Jodi is a special woman, and I count myself blessed. She brings out the best in me, although I still don't make the bed to her standard. But what made our wedding day even more special was having my close friend, Justin Pybas, as my best man. He is an attorney who graduated from the University of Oklahoma School of Law. He is a man with greater tenacity than most anyone I know. Having graduated near the top of his class when pursuing his undergraduate degree, he sat for the bar exam—scoring near the top percentile of all test takers in America. Although he was offered a scholarship to attend law school at Boston University, he decided to put down roots in Oklahoma and instead accepted a full-tuition scholarship to the state's oldest school of law. Today he works with a major firm in Oklahoma and is one of the most intelligent men I know.

Justin and I actually met in seventh grade, where we were both substandard members of the wrestling team. I believe that if wrestling was a requirement for public education graduation, we would have both flunked out. Despite our obvious deficiencies for hand-to-hand combat, I could tell even then that Justin was a person of character. Later in life, we crossed paths when, during high school, we both played a sport we were more suited for—soccer. But it wasn't until we again crossed paths in the same church youth group that we became friends. Over these past fifteen years or so we have shared a lot of experiences, but first among them is supporting each other.

Trying to "keep up" with Justin has made me stronger. In certain areas of his life I look up to him. When he was just twenty-five years old, he was asked to serve as a deacon of our church, a post usually reserved for the elders of the congregation, while I struggle just to stay on the path. He excelled in school through pure hard work, where I was prone to coast on my confidence in my intelligence. And Justin is dedicated, recently completing a marathon "just because" he wanted to overcome a challenge. I've gained 15 pounds since I have been married—sorry, honey!

"Leaders consciously surround themselves with people of great expectation"

Because Justin is in my life, I still play soccer every week and that keeps me in better shape than I would be otherwise. Because Justin is in my life, I am encouraged to follow God more than walking alone. And because Justin is in my life, I work hard to increase my knowledge, not just coast on my ego. I don't take intelligence for granted over knowledge and wisdom.

To find success as an emerging leader, you must sharpen yourself on the strengths of your fellowships. Those friends, family, and colleagues that you associate with determine the speed of your development. Surrounding yourself with men and women of character, those with drive and ambition and those with a genuine concern for your success is vital to your own achievements. Very few people of greatness achieved it without the help of many. Can you count on those in your life to demand the very best of you? To push you when you want to settle for mediocrity? Surround yourself with those of great expectation and great character. Iron sharpens iron, as one man sharpens another.

I enjoyed the positive experience of receiving the Republican nomination for the Oklahoma State House of Representatives when I was just twenty-four years old. I was to have represented the people of central and downtown Oklahoma City. The campaign represented a period of great challenge, growth, and enlightenment. I did not win the election, however. All of us face setbacks, and placing second in that race was one of my great disappointments—although I would do it all over again even if I knew in advance I would not win.

Joshua Fahrenbruck is another successful emerging leader; a man of towering passion who embodies the lesson of passion and knowledge. He was even cornerstone to growing a highly successful non-profit group dedicated to mentoring young professionals in Oklahoma with several hundred members—now that's passion. My friend Joshua is who approached me to ask that I run for the House of Representatives. He set aside his own ambition in order to see me succeed and see the community he cared for be better represented. Joshua did more than put my name in a hopper. He worked side by side for eighteen months with me, unpaid and with no complaints, to put the fuel behind the campaign. He was the passion that made me stronger. Iron sharpens iron, as one man sharpens another.

Dick and Mac McDonald were running McDonald's Hamburger Stand in California successfully. Just a small business that was selling fifteen-cent hamburgers. But when Ray Croc showed up, they began to franchise and build their business. Today they sell $21 billion dollars worth of those little hamburgers each year. Iron sharpens iron, as one man sharpens another.

When Express Personnel Services was founded by Bob Funk, Bill Stoller, and James Gray in 1983, the company began to grow. But James was afraid of losing the company culture and wanted to "cap" the number of locations at thirty sites. Bob and Bill decided to buyout James' shares of the company and build their dream together. In 2007, more than 375,000 people and their families will cash a paycheck from the job they found through Express Personnel. Had we stopped growing at thirty locations, that number would be around eighteen thousand people. Nearly 360,000 more people and their families were helped because iron sharpens iron, as one man sharpens another.

Surround yourself with the best people you can find. End relationships with those who want you to settle. Just as I work to sharpen Justin and Joshua, you must support those people made of iron in your life, and they will in turn sharpen you. You will both get better, just as iron sharpens iron.

So I challenge you to take an account of your relationships and do one of the hardest things in life that is necessary to emerge as a leader. You will only sharpen as you surround yourself with iron. *Today* is the day to end relationships that cause you to settle for mediocrity. Today is the day to end relationships that dull your success. You take an important step toward your emergence when you decide, and act, to only invest in relationships that sharpen you.

Conclusions

You are an emerging leader with a bright future. I know after learning these eight lessons your abilities have already improved and that alone is to be applauded. So here is to you racehorse, I know you are going to surpass all expectations.

You have learned the critical importance of eliminating any attitude of entitlement and will play well enough to beat the other team and the referee. Working as a racehorse sets you apart while you protect yourself from loose woodpeckers. Initial success will not turn you toward fastidiousness. With intimidation you will be reminded of the vulnerability of even our greatest heroes. You continue to learn the power of knowledge and passion as the keys to gaining influence. Decisions made in a vacuum are the worst decisions you can make, just as making moves in chess without taking into account your opponent will surely result in losses. All this cannot be accomplished without support, and building your network of supporters is the only path to sustaining success.

Mastering the eight lessons of *The Emerging Leader* cannot be accomplished in a lifetime. Remember that "we never arrive," and that applies to these lessons as well. However, just ask yourself, "Did I do better today than I did yesterday?" The answer better be "Yes."

About the Author

Despite growing up in very humble beginnings and admittedly performing mediocre in school, David Lewis soon began to emerge as a leader. His career began as a pharmacist and physician recruiter, serving clients including Eckerd, Walgreens, Kmart, as well as dozens of major hospitals. Lewis then served on Capitol Hill in Washington D.C. for a ranking congressman, and, upon returning to Oklahoma, he received nomination to the State House of Representatives. He is an appointee to advise the governor of the State of Oklahoma on workforce and economic development matters, and by 2006 he had built a $10 million business unit for the largest privately held staffing company in America while at the same time growing his own rental property company. Lewis has been featured in dozens of radio, television, and print appearances as an expert on human resources and leadership. Then he turned twenty-six.

David Lewis has been awarded as one of Oklahoma's "40 most accomplished business leaders under 40" by the *Journal Record*. *Oklahoma City Business* called him "one of our most admired young business leaders." He has been cited regionally and nationally as an expert on career development and human resources. Lewis is part of an elite group recognized as a "Senior Professional in Human Resources" by the Society for Human Resource Management. He lives in Piedmont, Oklahoma, with his wife, Jodi, herself a successful emerging leader.

David and Jodi Lewis